GW00542474

Astrology Art

Copyright © Therrie Rosenvald-Schmidt & Marc Waldemar Schmidt 2004

All rights reserved. No part of this publication may be reproduced, stored in or introduced into a retrieval system, or transmitted in any form or by any means (electronic, mechanical, photocopying, recording or otherwise) without written permission of the publisher. Any person who does any unauthorised act in relation to this publication may be liable to criminal prosecution and civil claims for damages.

2nd Edition 2004
1st Edition published 2001

ISBN 1-877063-02-9

Published by
Astrology Art
24 Wallace Road
Beachmere 4510
Queensland, Australia

Printed in Singapore by PH Productions Pte Ltd

The Versatile Gemini

Text by Therrie Rosenvald-Schmidt

Illustrations by Marc Waldemar Schmidt

General

There's one thing a Gemini isn't and that is boring. As the third sign of the Zodiac, Gemini rules the House of Communication and boy, do these people love to talk. They spend hours on the phone. With charm and wit they will extract every little bit of knowledge from all the people they meet. It's not just small talk with these people either. The strength behind the Geminian conversation is their agile mind.

People born under this sign are intellectual explorers, forever probing people and places in search of information. The more information a Gemini collects, the better. The typical Gemini is a fountain of knowledge and knows something about everything. If they don't have any data on a specific topic you'll never notice because with their quick minds they can bluff their way through. Collecting information is only half the fun for the Gemini. This sign loves to share the information later on with friends, family and partners.

It is often said that Geminis are flippant about love. They aren't really, it just appears that way. Geminis are secretive about their inner feelings and often don't even admit them to themselves. Maybe there's a deep-rooted fear that admitting being in love will curb their independence. Freedom and independence are top priorities for the Gemini. In an ideal Gemini world marriage or any other personal relationships will slot nicely in between all their other activities and interests, which multiply every day. These people don't want to be accountable to their partners for every minute of the day. Nagging, making scenes because they smiled at the neighbour and demanding absolute attention are the quickest way to scare them off. Geminis expect their partners to trust them, and if they feel that marriage is an expansion of their horizon they will happily commit and stay faithful.

As a mutable sign Geminis are extremely flexible and can adapt to any change in circumstances in an instant. The Gemini will set out to buy a pair of socks and come home with load of timber. What happened? Well, on the way Gemini had the bright idea of building a cubby house for the kids. And this is one person who has to react immediately. They can't sit still for the briefest of moments and as the sign of the Twins they're forever doing ten things simultaneously.

Since Geminis are a mix of the yin and yang, they are well represented by the Twins . Gemini people easily see both sides of an issue, a wonderful practical quality. Less practical is that one is never sure which Twin has the upper hand. This often makes them fickle and restless. With the Twins alternating control, Geminis often appear to be wishy-washy with a habit of changing their minds and moods on a simple whim. However, life with a Gemini is always a lot of fun. Geminis are bright, quick-witted and will liven up any get-together. Their ideas and imagination are light years ahead of the rest of the world.

Gemini Female

If you're the possessive type stay away from the Gemini woman. This is one girl who has so many outside interests, you'll have to make an appointment well in advance to see her. But she's as bubbly as French champagne, quick-witted, charming and fun. Gemini women are constantly running to some exciting event. You won't catch the Twin girl at home alone, feeling sorry for herself and moaning that she's bored. If she gets bored, she'll do something about it quick smart and if a suitor bores her, she'll be gone in a flash. Gemini is not a sign that lets the grass grow under their feet. If they want to do something, they'll do it now.

If you have chosen a Gemini girl to spend the rest of your life with be prepared for a lively adventure. You'll hardly have time to breath trying to keep pace with her. Her appointment book is crammed full with things she wants to do or see and every morning she adds a few more to the list. This is a girl that's sizzling with energy.

As an air sign the Gemini female's brain ticks over at 200 miles per hour every minute of the day. And what a brain it is. You can talk about anything with a Gemini, whether it's nuclear physics or politics, she's never lost for words. If she hasn't got a clue what you're talking about you will never know, because she's a master at giving the impression that she knows what she's talking about.

The Gemini woman won't smother her children with protection. She will be eager to feed her offspring's minds just as regularly as their stomachs.

Gemini Male

The Gemini man will entangle any female with charm and vivacity so quickly her head will spin. Just when she's ready to abandon everything near and dear to her, to ride off into the sunset with the charismatic Twin, he'll see someone else and do the same to her. Is Gemini too fickle or a Don Juan or just downright cruel? Actually he's none of these. Gemini happens to spread his charm to any female. He loves flirting and finding out what makes other people tick. His mind runs like a well maintained racing machine and being charming and flirtatious is part of his nature.

Maybe you got it all wrong and he just wanted to be friends. It's really hard to figure out the Gemini's intentions. Maybe it's because the Gemini hasn't got a clue what his intentions are either. One minute he's just about ready to go down on bended knees and pop the question, the next minute he's hardly aware that you exist.

Geminis are intrigued by mysterious things and people. It's best to feed the Gemini man only titbits of information and keep him in suspense. But be warned, it's not easy to mentally outmanoeuvre a Gemini. He's got the mental agility of a rattle snake and will tie your mind into knots. Before you know it you'll be spilling the beans. You've got to be on your toes all the time.

The Gemini man is a kid at heart, no matter what age. He'll fill the house with gimmicks and toys and spend hours in shopping centres, discovering all the new things to play with. He's also great with the kids and will keep them entertained for hours on end. He's just a dish.

Ambitions

The Gemini's big ambition is to see all and experience all. They dream about living one lifetime after another, preferably in every century for the next 500 years. Their misfortune is that they have only one body and there is too much to see for just one person in a single lifetime.

With the Gemini's versatile brain they see infinite possibilities for everything. They spend a lot of time imagining what could be if this and that would happen. No one plays the 'if only' game as frequently as the Twins.

For Geminis success is all about lifestyle and mental development. This is a sign that doesn't give two hoots about money or status. Money is only important because it can buy freedom. Geminis have so much wit, mental agility and charm that the doors to society open automatically. Therefore they have absolute no use for status.

For the Twins success is all about freedom. They feel successful if they have the personal freedom to come and go as they please, the financial freedom to be able to afford all the toys that take their fancy and the emotional freedom to not have to live up to someone else's expectations and be forced to make commitments they are not yet ready for. Most of all success means freedom of thought. Being hemmed in, in any sort of way, travelling through life on set tracks would be the Twins' worst nightmare.

People born under this sign want to take deep breaths, stretch their legs and know that they can head off in any direction they like, preferably all of them at the same time. They haven't got time sitting around, thinking about what they want to do, they just do it and see what happens.

Love Match Gemini & Gemini

You won't find a more versatile, charming, or vivacious pair. These two will never bore each other, for they are interested in everything. The pace is reckless and that's the way they like it. This couple will also never run out of interesting things to talk about, they have tons of friends, and they'll create some spectacular amusement. Sex is fun and games. The only problem this couple will have, is curbing the restlessness and settling down to mundane domesticity.

Geminis juggle so many things at the same time,
it's confusing and exhausting just to watch them.

Career

Geminis can only be happy in a career that offers plenty of freedom. A job that demands that they work in one environment for any length of time, is unsuitable for the Twins. These are not people who can clock on at the exact same time every morning, year in, year out. Even thinking about such medieval working conditions can make Geminis nauseous.

Geminis need lots of variety and new experiences. In younger years they will try out many jobs to see what suits them best. They manage to compile quite a colourful resume until they have found the ideal career path with the right mixture of fun, challenges and excitement. Geminis are born communicators, and a career talking to lots of people is ideal for them. They make fabulous talkshow hosts or news presenters and journalists. As Travel writers or foreign correspondents they meet new people, new cultures and make new experiences almost on a daily basis. Best of all, they get paid for communicating all they have learnt to others.

Many Geminis do branch out on their own, but not necessarily to start up a new company. Geminis love freelance work. The freedom to pick and choose their jobs and working hours is like a dream come true. Working their own hours allows Geminis to browse through the shopping centres during the day and checking out all that is new. And at night, instead of sleeping, they will be burning the midnight oil to catch up on their workload.

As employers Geminis relate well to their employees on a one-on-one basis. They will suss out each special talent. Being tied down to a company, with all the responsibilities, is often too constricting for Twins and they delegate work to various members of their team. Freeing up their own time allows Geminis to explore new possibilities, make new contacts and talk to new people. Of course, its all for business.

Love Match Gemini & Cancer

Passionate Cancer fulfils Gemini's physical needs, and Gemini's cheerfulness brightens Cancer's moody disposition. However, Gemini's flippant approach to love and the tendency to flirt will undermine the Cancerian need for security. Also independent Gemini won't respond well to Cancer's possessiveness. Cancer craves domesticity and Gemini loathes it. Cancer needs to curb the moodiness, and Gemini needs to treat Cancer with more sensitivity.

Versatility is the trademark of the Gemini character. There are so many sides to the Twins, it's not easy to figure out the real person.

Family

A Gemini parent is mostly fun, but can also be very confusing sometimes. Geminis are lively spirits, constantly reinventing themselves. For a young child, who needs consistency, this can be a bit puzzling. Gemini parents may have different views today as they had yesterday. On the plus side, life is never dull with Gemini parents, as they enthusiastically embrace their children's adventures.

Geminis are not interested in creating small replicas of themselves and won't have a long list of ground rules to follow. They are pretty gung-ho about discipline. Actually, Geminis will be the first to applaud and encourage differences in their children's characters and views. In the Gemini household everyone, no matter how young, has a right to their own opinions. Gemini parents will never order a child to do exactly as told. On the contrary, they respect their children's individuality and know that the best they can do is guide them to the right choice.

As an air sign, Geminis cherish intellectual stimulation. They give their offspring the best education they can afford and will take an active part in forming the young mind without restricting it. There will be plenty of books available on every subject Junior has briefly shown an interest in. A more practical child will, however, challenge Gemini parents. There could be some struggle until parents and child have found a common denominator. However, Geminis are masters at accepting new things and will undoubtedly find a way to encourage their child's special talents, however strange these are to the Twins.

Geminis love toys and gadgets and will almost certainly have an impressive collection of both. They also love to play and will happily spend hours amusing their children. Though they can get a bit cranky when little fingers smear marmalade all over their collection of miniature cars. Geminis are never too tired or too busy to talk to their children. They are not overly physical and cuddles sometimes fall a bit short. But Gemini parents always take an active interest in every stage of their children's life.

Love Match Gemini & Leo

Gemini's playfulness will match well with extroverted Leo's sense of humour. Leo is just as independent and flirtatious as Gemini. Leo will thoroughly enjoy Gemini's biting humour as long as it's not at the big cat's expense. The only cloud in the sky will be that Leo wants more adoration than Gemini is willing to give. This is a good team, Gemini provides the ideas and Leo has the stamina to see projects through to the end and they will have loads of fun doing it.

Movement and speed are Gemini's great passion. The Twins don't believe in travelling through life in the slow lane.

Friendship

Twins make new friends every day of the week. They chat up people in supermarkets, parking lots and even traffic jams. This is a sign that has an insatiable need for new faces and new perspectives. People born under this sign pop in and out of other people's lives like yoyos. One minute they're there, the next they are gone. Geminis have friends from just about every walk of life, race, creed and age group. A variety of different people, with different opinions and knowledge, stimulate Geminis' intellectual juices.

Geminis look to their friends for companionship and the sharing of ideas. They can hang on the phone for hours, exchanging views about everything, from the latest diet fad to the state of the world economy. Geminis are a minefield of information and up-to-date on all the juiciest gossip, new trends and bargains.

No one can counter a snide remark as quickly as Geminis, and with such charm and wit. They can breath life into the most boring social event, which is one of the reasons they are usually invited to every party in town. Geminis have a curious mind and will probe into the deepest crevices of their new friend's life. Once the Twins know everything about a person and there is nothing new to discover, they will move onto more interesting subjects. People, who can uphold a friendship with Geminis over many years, must have very interesting characters.

Nothing can put Geminis off as quickly as possessiveness. A friendship with someone who is clingy and jealous doesn't last very long. Geminis need to feel free and independent and being hampered by too many restrictions irritates them and makes them want to run. The most annoying part of a friendship with Geminis is that they are never on time and occasionally forget appointments. They don't really do it on purpose, they just get so easily sidetracked on the way.

Love Match Gemini & Virgo

Gemini and Virgo are both Mercury-ruled and have a mental approach to life. Despite their apparent similarity, they differ in their outlook. Life is no joke for serious Virgo, whereas Gemini thinks life is too short to waste on worrying and concentrates on having fun. It won't do Gemini any harm to slow down occasionally and listen to what Virgo has to say, and Virgo could greatly benefit by learning to enjoy the mischief Gemini constantly creates.

Geminis are restless characters and if you try to pin them down for longer than ten seconds, they vanish into thin air.

Health

Staying fit is usually not much of an issue for Geminis. They are constantly rushing back and forth from one place to another. Geminis live on their nerves and burn up energy for at least two people. Distracted by their inquisitive minds, they often forget to eat or sleep. For Geminis the day is never long enough to do all the things planned or for that matter, unplanned.

The sign of Gemini rules the nervous system and mental and nervous exhaustion are common occurrences amongst the Twins. Problems with the shoulders and arms are typical for the Geminis. Muscle tension, especially in the shoulder region, should be treated with gentle massages before it 'freezes'. Geminis usually ignore the messages their bodies hand out. This results in a weakened immune system and that makes them more susceptible to colds and flues. The lungs also fall into the Gemini's domain and they need to especially guard against chest infections.

When Geminis do get sick, one virtually needs to tie them to the bed so that they can recuperate. It is during this time that their moody, unresponsive side comes to the forefront. Because inactivity is so foreign to Geminis, they will snap at everyone, even the cat, for no reason at all. The longer they are confined to bed, the more irritable they get.

Geminis would greatly benefit from relaxation techniques, if they can stay still for more than two minutes. This would teach them to slow down and unblock their minds. Proper breathing methods support relaxation, which calms the spirit. It is also advisable that Geminis make an effort to eat regularly and get enough sleep. The world will still be here tomorrow.

Love Match Gemini & Libra

These two air signs are well suited. They are stimulating companions who will enjoy a light-hearted, enchanting affair. Neither is aggressive and they think alike. Both are affectionate, fun-loving and enjoy an active social life. Their passions are enthusiastic, neither is jealous nor demanding. Libra won't mind Gemini's taste for experiments. The finances may be in a bit of a mess most of the time and the need to buckle down will dampen the spirits occasionally.

Geminis have clever ideas to make everyday life easier. Maybe one day they'll invent something the world has been waiting for.

Holidays

It seems as if Geminis are always on holidays. They have such a strong need to get away from the routine of daily life that they will organise themselves a succession of mini-holidays throughout the year. These can range from a couple of hours in the shopping mall to a few days at a Formula One Racing Carnival, or just a weekend in another city.

If there is a public holiday coming up, Gemini will be the first to request a few extra days off before and after the official holiday. It is not surprising that Geminis use up all their allotted holiday time and need to take a few weeks unpaid annual leave. Standby and today-only holiday specials were made for Gemini people. When they decide they need a change of scenery, which is about every other week, they will drop everything and head off to the airport, their favourite mode of travel. Geminis like short bursts of getaways and preferably to an exciting place. No secluded island for these people. A quick trip to New York or Hong Kong is perfect for them.

Geminis don't mind travelling with others as long as they don't feel restricted in their movements. As they constantly dash off into another direction, taking organised tours is not for them. Geminis absolutely hate assembly-line tourism and won't put up with being bustled from one must-see tourist spot to the other.

Twins are sociable people and they want to get to know everything about their host country. They'll talk to the locals, visit the places not listed in the brochures and learn about new ideas and cultures. They will, however, have favourite destinations, which they visit frequently.

For Gemini getting to their destination is not as exciting as arriving there and they have an uncanny knack of finding out the fastest possible route from point A to point B. Stopovers are hardly ever used, unless there is something interesting to see and experience. Geminis prefer to keep on the move. There is so much to see and so little time left.

Love Match Gemini & Scorpio

The match of imagination and dynamic is quite exhilarating. Gemini and Scorpio complement each other if they learn to get along together. The physical relationship will be astonishing, to say the least. This is not a couple burdened by inhibitions. Scorpio must learn to curb the jealousy and possessiveness otherwise Gemini's free spirit will be on the run. Gemini's frivolous attitude towards love won't be appreciated by Scorpio and some conflicts may arise.

Feeding an immensely curious nature, Geminis are willing to
try just about anything from deep sea diving to air acrobatics.

Humour

There hardly is a sign that has a quicker wit than Gemini. As they rule communication, Geminis use language in very original ways to provoke laughs. Parties and other social gatherings are always good opportunities to practice their word games and their quick-witted sense of humour. Anyone who is anxious about entertaining their guests, need not worry if a Gemini is invited. With the Twins present at the dinner table, there will never be any embarrassing silent moments.

Geminis have a highly sophisticated sense of humour and sometimes only the sharpest minds can pick up the punch line. They are keen observers of human nature and quickly discover how to make fun of peculiar idiosyncrasies. Twins can mimic almost anyone. With their fine hearing, they pick up every nuance of speech and can recreate it perfectly. They are also masters at reading body language and quickly discover any insecurities or hidden secrets.

For Geminis, life would be a dreary existence without their sense of humour. It plays an important role in all aspects of their life. Even when things are not going too well, they will try to see the funny side of life. Geminis don't really like to reveal their weaknesses and they will often hide their insecurities behind humour. They are also highly skilled in wriggling themselves out of sticky situations with a witty remark.

Though there are times when their sunny disposition deserts them, this usually happens when their dark Twin is in control and they stumble into one of their black moods. If they are still capable of displaying a sense of humour, it will be very sarcastic.

Making fun of situations and people's habits is an enjoyable game for Geminis. If they are on a roll, or the evil Twin is popping to the forefront, Geminis may go a bit too far and forget their target's feelings. They don't mean to be nasty, they just can't resist a good laugh. However, with their immense charm they will immediately make things right again. As much as Geminis enjoy a laugh at the expense of others, they find it hard to laugh at themselves.

Love Match Gemini & Sagittarius

Now here's a match that will go down in the history books. With fun-loving Gemini and boisterous Sagittarius there won't ever be a dull moment. Both have wide-ranging and varied interests. Sagittarius tends to be more intellectual, Gemini more social. They are restless, argumentative and in need of a lot of freedom. Gemini will find the Sagittarian's verbal goofs very amusing. Neither are too demonstrative with emotions. Humour is the key for these two.

Geminis are normally kind and compassionate, but they also have a mischievous streak and sometimes the little devil emerges.

Lovers

There is not much Geminis take seriously in life and that includes love. For these people, it's all about having fun and getting a few good laughs, not complicated emotions. If the lovemaking with a partner is exciting and entertaining they'll stick around. Geminis are not the most faithful sign of the Zodiac. As soon as it becomes routine and boring, they'll cast their glances elsewhere. After all, there are plenty of other fish swimming in the big sea, some of which are already dazzling the Twins with brilliant colours from afar.

Geminis are born flirts and they can't help showing off their quick wit to every member of the opposite sex, who crosses their path. Most of the time, this is just innocent banter, not to be taken seriously. However, it is often misconstrued and Geminis continually get themselves into some very sticky situations.

Variety is the spice of life, and Geminis like plenty of it in the bedroom. They will not be too shy to introduce some fun adult toys and delight in discovering their different effects. Geminis like to have an imaginative sex life. They'll try just about any position and do it anywhere. With Geminis, lovemaking doesn't start and end in the bedroom. They'll be well engaged in their foreplay with witty remarks and erotic chatter many hours before. Talking is an important part of Gemini's lovemaking tactics. Pillow talk, amusing anecdotes and jokes, in between or during and after the actual act, make it unique every time. The only thing Geminis have a problem with, is confessing their feelings of love. Even at the climax of sexual pleasure they will not scream out "I love you!".

Now this does not mean they don't feel it, it's just they wouldn't recognise love if it hits them in the face. They don't want to discuss or even think about feelings. If they feel comfortable with someone that's all that matters. However, if their love life is interesting, and they don't feel restricted or obligated, and don't get a dirty look or lecture every time they smile at someone new, then being in a relationship is not that bad.

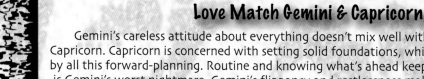

Love Match Gemini & Capricorn

Gemini's careless attitude about everything doesn't mix well with steady, conservative Capricorn. Capricorn is concerned with setting solid foundations, while Gemini feels threatened by all this forward-planning. Routine and knowing what's ahead keep Capricorn happy, but this is Gemini's worst nightmare. Gemini's flippancy and restlessness make Capricorn feel insecure. With Gemini's imagination and Capricorn's persistency, these two can be very successful.

Communication is Gemini's primary talent, and do they love to talk.
They spend hours on the phone discussing anything and everything.

Marriage

Getting Gemini to the altar is no easy task. They want to stay footloose and fancy free and at the slightest hint of the "M" word one only sees a dust cloud on the horizon. Marriage is for many Geminis synonymous with receiving a life sentence. They also have a big problem choosing the right partner, because there are so many to choose from and who knows what is just around the next corner.

Now this does not mean that Geminis never get married. Sometimes curiosity gets the better of them and they decide to give it a try. There is rarely a lot of planning beforehand. Geminis want the wedding to be a quick affair. A drive-through marriage ceremony, with a few burgers thrown in, would be perfect for them. Geminis don't spend a lot of time analysing their marriage. If there are problems, time will hopefully solve them. If not, well, divorce isn't such a big deal either. For Twins marriage isn't everything in life, it either works or it doesn't.

They don't want to spend time and money on self-help books and marriage counsellors. Even with a ring on their finger, Geminis won't see anything wrong with some harmless flirting with members of the opposite sex. It rarely amounts to much more than friendly chitchat, unless there is something wrong with the marriage. When the laughs stop and talking develops into a verbal slinging match with accusations flying back and forth, Gemini's marriage is in serious trouble. If they aren't happy, Geminis look for greener pastures and won't feel guilty if they stray.

Friendship, companionship, a sharing of interests and communication are the fabrics that make a Gemini marriage successful. The spouse of a Gemini has to be flexible and independent. There is nothing Geminis hate more than a partner who stifles them. They don't want to account for their whereabouts 24/7. If their partners give them plenty of breathing space, trust them, the Twins will be happy and the marriage will last and be heaps of fun.

Love Match Gemini & Aquarius

This is one crazy couple and they will create some havoc together. They like experimenting, discovering new worlds and new ideas. Both are unpredictable and life will often become turbulent. Aquarius adores Gemini's sense of fun and Gemini finds the Aquarian eccentricity amusing. Both are fiercely independent and neither is bothered by the other's restlessness. Gemini may occasionally utter a sarcastic remark about Aquarius' ideals, but its all in good fun.

Geminis can browse through shops for hours, looking at everything, touching everything, and are not shy to sample the odd product.

Pets

A hectic lifestyle and a social calendar bursting at the seams, plus the million and one other little things that grab the Gemini's attention, does not leave much time for the care of a pet. Geminis forget to feed themselves, let alone feed a pet. A placid, tranquil dog that waits patiently in the corner until he is fed, could starve in the Gemini's household.

Cats are far better equipped to make sure the Twins don't forget their needs. They can meow incessantly and are hard to ignore. Cats are very much like Geminis, once their belly is full, they too will forget their human companion, just as Geminis forget them. Occasionally, Geminis crave attention and cats can be very responsive when they're in the mood for some stroking and cuddling. Geminis find the sleek movements and slender body of a cat immensely attractive. A short hair cat, possibly Siamese would be the perfect feline choice.

Geminis need a lot of freedom and being tied to a demanding four-legged friend is not an ideal situation for them. They'd loathe a dog that is constantly at their heels and slobbering all over their clothes and numerous toys. Even the thought of the sheer hard work in taking care of any large animal, such as a horse, would be enough to send the Twins packing. Gemini farmers are as scarce as hen's teeth, unless of course, they've got dozens of labourers doing the work.

Being an air sign, Geminis take a liking to birds. If they can talk, such as parrots or parakeets, Gemini is in seventh heaven. Just imagine the pure bliss of the Twins, who adore talking more than any other sign, being able to tell Polly the parrot everything they have experienced that day. The only problem is that Polly will indiscriminately blab out all Gemini's secrets to whom ever takes the time to listen.

Love Match Gemini & Pisces

Mystical Pisces fascinates Gemini and Pisces will adore Gemini's playfulness. Pisces is sensitive and easily hurt if Gemini is too flippant about feelings. Neither are good at dealing with everyday things, Gemini is bored by responsibility and Pisces is frightened of it. Gemini needs independence and Pisces needs reassurance. Pisces will struggle to feel secure with restless Gemini, and Gemini will feel hemmed in by Pisces' clinginess.

All kinds of gadgets light up the Gemini heart. Their homes and offices are cluttered with things that make life more efficient.

Style

Geminis have better things to do than worry about their appearance. They usually grab whatever is handy and clean, then head out the door. It doesn't surprise anyone to see Geminis with two different coloured socks or wearing a jumper back to front. With their minds racing ahead, they rarely take the time to throw even a quick glance in the mirror before running off to something new.

Despite their lack of attention to fashion, Geminis are mostly well dressed. They seem to have a knack of throwing things together without a thought, and still somehow get it right. They prefer a streamlined, sporty style with a touch of classic, but it is always casual. One hardly ever sees Geminis in formal dress or a suit and tie. With their slender physiques, Geminis wear clothes rather well. The secret behind their successful fashion formula is that they are particularly good at mixing and matching. Without much fuss they make their outfits part of their personality. Geminis keep the volume of their wardrobe at a two suitcase, maximum three, limit. When they are ready to move on, it has to be quick. They are more inclined to leave everything behind than waste time packing up.

Geminis choose clothing that can be worn with lots of different things. By adding accessories, they are masters at dressing something up or down. The same piece of clothing has to be suitable for a business meeting, as well as a night out on the town. Geminis just love the reversible jacket concept and wish that everything else could also be turned inside out, therefore creating completely different looks from a few choice pieces. Of course, everything in the Gemini's wardrobe is made from easy-care fabric that they can throw into the washing machine and never needs ironing.

At home, Geminis need variety and are bored with a particular interior design very quickly. Some Geminis put all their furniture on wheels so that they can easily move them around without much ado. They also prefer module furniture, just in case they want to move house. The overall picture of the Gemini's home is comfortable, stylish and simple, but terribly cluttered.

Love Match Gemini & Aries

Nobody will get a word in with this pair. They both love to talk and they're both frivolous in life and love. Gemini is just as restless and eager for new challenges as Aries and neither is afraid of new experiences. Gemini is clever enough to give Aries freedom. The word possessiveness doesn't exist in Gemini's vocabulary. On the contrary, Gemini is even more prone to seek outside stimulation than Aries, which may irritate Aries as the Ram wants to be first priority.

Geminis want to walk on new planets and communicate with beings far beyond our solar system. The Twin's imagination knows no limits.

Wealth

Geminis want to get rich today, not tomorrow when they are old and can't enjoy it anymore. If they could have it their way, they would decree that people enter retirement at the age of 20 and start their working career when they're 45 and work until they drop dead or pay off the 'early' retirement fund. This is not a sign that will devise a financial plan in their youth and stick to it for the next few decades. Piling dollar upon dollar until it grows to a big mountain is far too boring for them.

Geminis refuse to accept that wealth can only be built over long periods of time. They believe they only need one lucky break. Understandably, these are the most likely people to get sucked in by the various 'get-rich-quick' schemes, sometimes more than once. It can even happen that they outsmart the organisers and manage to grab their fortunes. Geminis fly by the seat of their pants. They'll enter into dubious speculative ventures or buy strange stock. Sometimes they land on their backsides and sometimes they win. Failure doesn't depress Geminis. If they lose, they will do something else.

Lotto and other games of chance, where the top prize is worth at least a million, will entice the Twins to buy tickets regularly. Since they get bored with the same thing all the time and patience isn't really one of their strong points, they tend to switch numbers often. It has happened that Geminis had all the right numbers the week before it hit the jackpot. But Geminis don't really need Lotto or a dodgy scheme to become wealthy. With their versatility and their lively imagination they are very well equipped to create their own destiny. Many Twins have earned a fortune by inventing a great product or by having invested in an obscure company a few years back, which has now made a scientific break through.

The big, fat bank account is far less important to Geminis than the personal and financial freedom it offers. For Geminis money is a commodity, something to trade for far more interesting things, such as travel, fast cars, mobile phones and many more toys for grown-ups.

Love Match Gemini & Taurus

These two are opposites in temperament and outlook on life. Taurus is resistant to change, whereas Gemini needs change to breath. Although they'll find each other intriguing at first, they will have to compromise. Gemini is attracted to Taurean's passions and Taurus enjoys Gemini's fun-loving nature. If Taurus can give Gemini some space and Gemini accepts Taurus's down-to-earth input, these two might build up a solid and bright future.

Geminis are the kids of the Zodiac and never lose the ability to laugh, play and enjoy every second of life, no matter what age.

Famous Geminis

22.05.1907	Sir Laurence Olivier, Actor
23.05.1883	Douglas Fairbanks, Sr., Actor
24.05.1941	Bob Dylan, Singer & Songwriter
25.05.1803	Ralph W. Emerson, Author, Poet, Philosopher
26.05.1886	Al Jolson, Broadway Star
27.05.1923	Henry Kissinger, US Secretary of State, Nobel Prize Winner
28.05.1968	Kylie Minogue, Singer
29.05.1917	John F. Kennedy, US President
30.05.1908	Mel Blanc, Voice Actor for cartoon figures
31.05.1908	Don Ameche, Actor
01.06.1926	Marilyn Monroe, Actress
02.06.1890	Hedda Hopper, Gossip Columnist
03.06.1906	Josephine Baker, Entertainer & Humanitarian
04.06.1971	Noah Wyle, Actor
05.06.1949	Ken Follet, Author of "Eye of the Needle"
06.06.1956	Bjorn Borg, Tennis Champion
07.06.1952	Liam Neeson, Actor
08.06.1933	Joan Rivers, TV Personality
09.06.1961	Michael J. Fox, Actor
10.06.1922	Judy Garland, Singer & Actress
11.06.1935	Gene Wilder, Actor & Commedian
12.06.1929	Anne Frank, Holocaust Victim & Dutch Diarist
13.06.1953	Tim Allen, Actor & Commedian
14.06.1969	Steffi Graf, Tennis Champion
15.06.1963	Helen Hunt, Actress
16.06.1890	Stan Laurel, Commedian
17.06.1980	Venus Williams, Tennis Champion
18.06.1942	Paul McCartney, Singer

Notes:

....

....

....

....

....

....

....

....

....

....

....

Astrology Art